Incredible Journeys

Contents

Claire Llewellyn
Character illustrations by Jon Stuart

OXFORD

Are we nearly there?

Have you ever been on a long journey? Some of us travel long distances to visit family or when we go on holiday. Most of us travel by car, bus or train. Sometimes we take a boat or a plane. Planes can travel to the other side of the world in a single day.

Animals go on long journeys, too. At certain times of year, many animals travel thousands of kilometres to places where they can feed or **breed**. This is called *migration*. Animals don't take cars or planes – they swim, walk or fly!

Snow geese

Green moray eel

Reindeer

Finding the way

When we're travelling somewhere new, we use maps to **navigate**. Or we travel with someone who knows the way.

How do you think animals find the way?

These young African elephants will follow the older animals who know the way.

Most migrating animals travel together. The young learn the route from older animals who have done the journey before.

Snow geese flying south for the winter.

Migrating animals have amazing memories. They remember **landmarks** like rivers and mountains and use them to find their way.

Some animals have an extra sense. Something inside them works like a **compass** and keeps them on the right track.

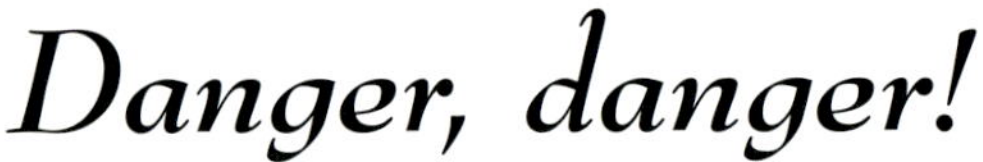

Danger, danger!

Migrating animals face many dangers.

Birds often have to face bad weather. Many go hungry and thirsty during their trip.

Some grazing animals migrate across the **grasslands** of Africa. They have to cross dangerous, fast-flowing rivers where they may be attacked by crocodiles.

Sea creatures may be attacked by predators or washed up on sandbanks.

A Nile crocodile tries to grab a migrating wildebeest.

Other dangers are caused by humans. Many animals are killed by poachers who hunt them illegally. At sea, migrating creatures can get stuck in fishing nets. Thousands of migrating birds are killed every year by flying into power lines.

Pollution can destroy the **habitat** a creature lives in or is travelling to. With nowhere to live, many animals will die.

A great white shark caught in a fishing net.

The swallow's journey

Swallows are small, fast-flying birds that feed on insects.

Every autumn, they migrate from Europe to South Africa. They cannot survive the winter in Europe because the insects they feed on die in the cold. So the birds fly south in small **flocks**. They navigate by the sun and an inner compass.

Swallows fly thousands of kilometres to find food in winter.

It is a long and hard journey. Only the strongest swallows reach South Africa. Here, they feed, rest and grow new feathers.

After a few months, the birds return to Europe where they will nest and breed. By then there are plenty of insects to feed their young.

A swallow feeding its young.

Swallow fact box

Journey	Europe to South Africa
Distance	10 000 kilometres
Departure	mid September
Return	mid March
Journey time	about 5 weeks
Number of migrations in lifetime	up to 10 return trips

The whale's voyage

Grey whales spend the winter in the warm waters near Mexico. The females give birth to their **calves** here. In spring, they begin to swim north to the Arctic where there is more food. The whales swim near the coast. They lift their heads to look for landmarks. This is called *spy-hopping*.

Look at that!

A grey whale leaps out of the water.

For the calves, it is a tiring and dangerous journey. They are vulnerable to attack by killer whales. With luck, they reach the icy Arctic waters where they can feed and grow. When autumn comes, they return south. By now the calves are strong enough for the long voyage back.

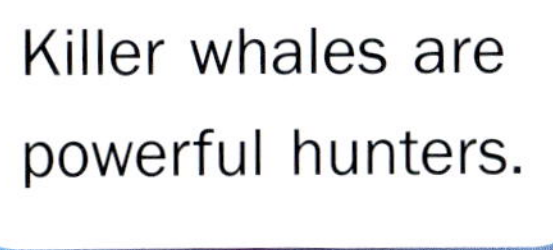

Killer whales are powerful hunters.

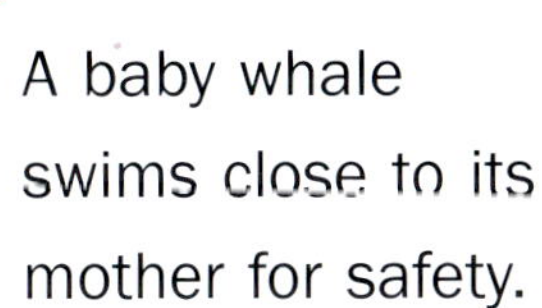

A baby whale swims close to its mother for safety.

Grey whale fact box

Journey	Mexico to the Arctic
Distance	8000 kilometres
Departure	February/March
Return	October
Journey time	2–3 months
Number of migrations in lifetime	up to 50 return trips

The salmon's homecoming

In spring, young salmon **hatch** in rivers all over Europe. The tiny fish live and grow in the river for a year. When they are about 10 centimetres long, they migrate downstream to the sea. They swim out into the Atlantic Ocean. They feed in the ocean for the next two or three years.

Did you know that baby salmon swim in groups called *schools*?

Salmon fact box

Journey	Atlantic Ocean to home river
Distance	7000 kilometres
Departure	July/August
Return	October/November
Journey time	over 2 months
Number of migrations in lifetime	up to 3 return trips

When the salmon are fully grown they return to their home river to breed. They swim or leap upstream against the flow of the water. They lay their eggs in the very spot where they hatched. How do they know they have found the right place? By the taste of the water!

An Atlantic salmon leaps upstream to return home.

The butterfly's flight

Monarch butterflies live in Canada. In September, before the weather turns cold, they fly south to Mexico. They ride on the wind and navigate by the sun. When they arrive in Mexico, they gather in a forest in the mountains. There they sink into a deep sleep.

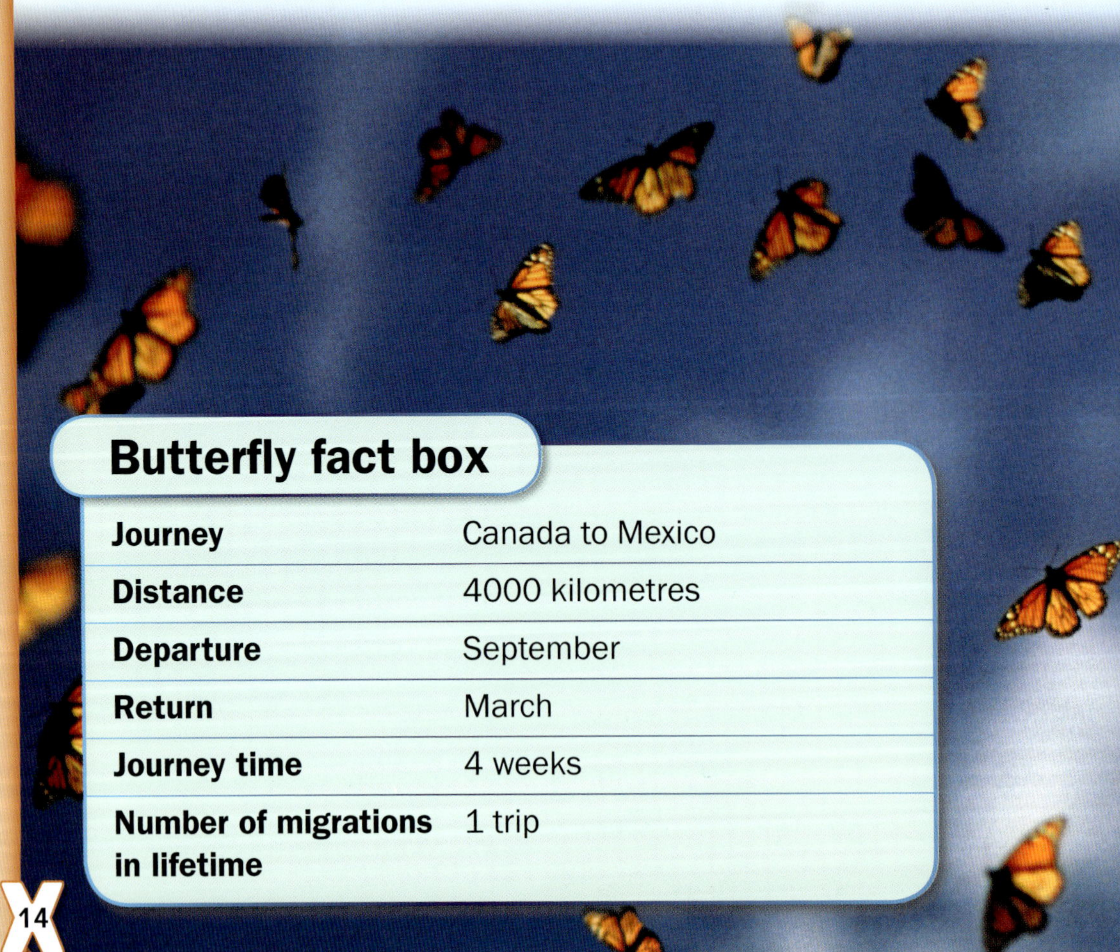

Butterfly fact box

Journey	Canada to Mexico
Distance	4000 kilometres
Departure	September
Return	March
Journey time	4 weeks
Number of migrations in lifetime	1 trip

Five months later, in spring, the butterflies wake up. They take to the air. Soon they begin to fly north again, laying eggs along the way. Butterflies have short lives and these adults will die before they reach Canada. The young that hatch from their eggs will fly on in their place.

The wildebeest's trek

Every year herds of wildebeest migrate in a huge circle around the grasslands of East Africa. The journey starts in Tanzania, in May, when the rains stop and the grass begins to die. The wildebeest trek north to Kenya to find food and water. They have to cross rivers where crocodiles lurk.

Six months later, the wildebeest return. They give birth to calves on the way home. The young must keep up with the adults or they will be hunted by lions or crocodiles. The animals travel day and night. At last they arrive in Tanzania where the rains have returned and the grass is growing again.

A newly-born wildebeest calf struggles to its feet – it must learn to run almost as soon as it is born.

Wildebeest fact box

Journey	Tanzania to Kenya to Tanzania
Distance	3000 kilometres
Departure	May
Return	November
Journey time	8 months
Number of migrations in lifetime	up to 20 trips

A male lion looking for food.

The turtle's return

Baby loggerhead turtles hatch on beaches on the south-east coast of America. The tiny animals quickly head for the water. It is a short but dangerous journey. They are attacked by foxes, rats and gulls that feast on the hatchlings. The surviving turtles enter the water and are swept out to sea.

For ten years the turtles travel in a huge circle around the Atlantic Ocean. Each animal travels alone, navigating by an inner compass.

It must be a very lonely journey!

Turtle fact box

Journey	around the North Atlantic Ocean
Distance	about 13 000 kilometres
Departure	after hatching
Return	May–August (10 years later)
Number of migrations in lifetime	10 or more

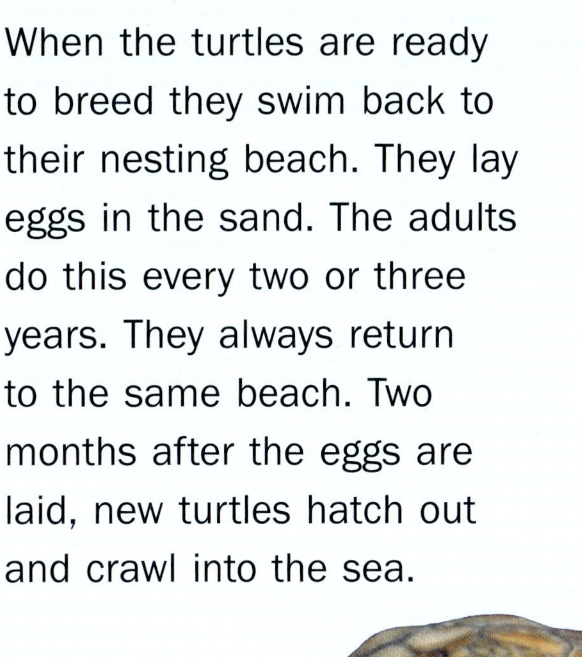

When the turtles are ready to breed they swim back to their nesting beach. They lay eggs in the sand. The adults do this every two or three years. They always return to the same beach. Two months after the eggs are laid, new turtles hatch out and crawl into the sea.

Female loggerhead turtle laying eggs.

Baby turtles heading for the sea.

Lending a hand

Humans sometimes cause problems for migrating animals but they can also help them. Scientists are finding out more about these animals and their journeys so they can try to protect them. The scientists fix tags to the animals. The tags give off signals that show exactly where the animals are.

This zebra is wearing a radio collar so scientists can track it.

Come on, this way!

A scientist in a microlight is showing some whooping cranes the way.

Some migrating animals are **endangered**. Whooping cranes have almost disappeared because their habitat has been destroyed. Scientists are trying to help them. They raise chicks during the spring and summer. In autumn, the birds need to migrate, but there are few adult cranes to lead them to their winter homes. So the scientists fly small planes to show the young birds the way.

World travellers

This map shows the incredible journeys made by the animals in this book.

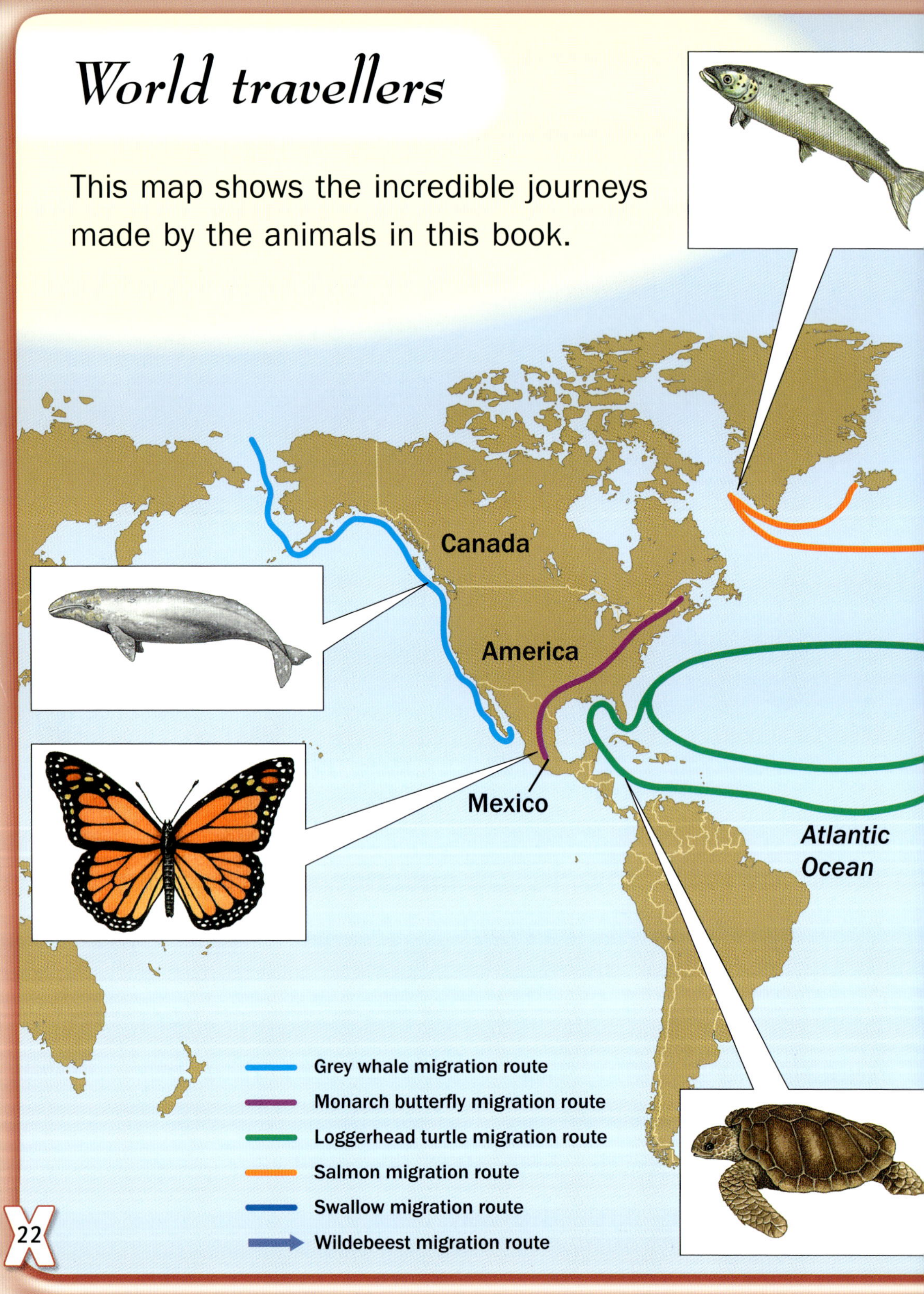

The Arctic
Europe
Africa
Kenya
Tanzania
East Africa
South Africa
N
W
E
S

Glossary

breed to produce young ones

calf a young whale, wildebeest, cow or elephant

compass an instrument with a needle that points north. It helps travellers to find their way

endangered in danger of dying out

flock a group of birds

grassland a large area of grass-covered land

habitat the place where an animal lives

hatch to break out of an egg

landmark a large object, like a hill or tower, that can be seen from a distance

navigate to find your way on a journey

Index